Dear Reade

This book invites you to walk with Jesus on His journey of love and sacrifice through the Stations of the Cross. Each station tells a powerful story of His courage, compassion, and ultimate gift for us all.

With simple descriptions, prayers, and child-friendly illustrations, this book helps children understand and reflect on Jesus' path to the cross and His resurrection.

Station I: Jesus Is Condemned to Death

Although Jesus was innocent, He was unfairly judged and sentenced to death. He accepted the unjust verdict with humility and love, knowing that He was fulfilling His Father's will.

Jesus, help me to face difficult times with patience and trust in You. Teach me to remember that You are always with me, even when I am treated unfairly.

Can I be forgiving and kind, even when someone misunderstands or judges me unfairly?

Station II: Jesus Takes Up His Cross

Jesus takes up His heavy cross with love and courage, knowing that this is the path chosen by His Father. Although it is difficult, He embraces it to show His great love for all of us.

Jesus, give me strength to carry the crosses in my life, no matter how small or big. Help me to trust in Your plan and to walk with courage, just as You did.

How can I carry my daily struggles with more patience and trust in Jesus?

Station III: Jesus Falls the First Time

Jesus, carrying the heavy cross, stumbles and falls to the ground. Despite the pain, He gets up and continues His journey, showing His great love and determination to save us all.

Jesus, when I feel weak and fall under the weight of my struggles, give me the strength to rise again and keep going. Help me to trust that You are always with me.

How can I rely on Jesus for strength when I face challenges in my life?

Station IV: Jesus Meets His Mother

As Jesus carries His heavy cross, He sees His mother Mary. She looks at Him with love and sorrow, giving Him the courage to continue His journey. Their hearts are united in suffering and love.

Jesus, thank You for the love of Mary, who shared in Your suffering. Help me to find comfort in my family and to bring comfort to others when they are in pain.

How can I show love and support to my family when they are struggling?

Station V: Simon of Cyrene Helps Jesus Carry His Cross

As Jesus struggles under the heavy cross, Simon of Cyrene steps forward to help Him. Simon's act of kindness reminds us to help others in their time of need.

Jesus, teach me to be kind and willing to help those who are struggling. Show me how to be a friend to those in need, just as Simon was a friend to You.

How can I be helpful and kind to someone who needs my support today?

Station VI: Veronica Wipes the Face of Jesus

As Jesus walks on the difficult path, Veronica steps forward with kindness and wipes His face with her cloth. Her brave act of compassion reminds us of the power of small, loving gestures.

Jesus, help me to see the needs of others and to respond with love and kindness. Teach me to be brave like Veronica, even when it's hard.

How can I show kindness and help someone who needs comfort today?

Station VII: Jesus Falls the Second Time

As Jesus walks the difficult path, He stumbles and falls again under the weight of suffering. Despite the pain, He rises, showing us the strength to persevere in the face of challenges.

Jesus, when I feel overwhelmed by my struggles, help me to rise and keep going. Teach me to trust in Your strength and love.

How can I find hope and strength when things feel too hard?

Station VIII: Jesus Meets the Women of Jerusalem

As Jesus carries the cross, He pauses to comfort the women of Jerusalem who are weeping for Him. His words of compassion remind us to think of others, even in our own struggles.

Jesus, help me to see the needs of others and to show them kindness and love, even when I face challenges. Teach me to follow Your example of selflessness.

How can I bring comfort and hope to someone who is sad or struggling today?

Station IX: Jesus Falls the Third Time

Exhausted and carrying the weight of the cross, Jesus falls for the third time. Despite the pain and exhaustion, He rises again, determined to complete His mission of love and sacrifice.

Jesus, when I feel like giving up, remind me of Your strength and perseverance. Help me to rise again and keep moving forward with faith.

How can I find the courage to keep going, even when it's hard?

Station X: Jesus Is Stripped of His Garments

As Jesus reaches Golgotha, the soldiers strip Him of His garments. He endures this humiliation with dignity, teaching us humility and the importance of self-sacrifice.

Jesus, help me to let go of my pride and accept moments of humility with grace. Teach me to trust in Your love during difficult times.

How can I practice humility and show love to others today?

Station XI: Jesus Is Nailed to the Cross

Jesus willingly lays down on the cross as the soldiers prepare to nail His hands and feet. Despite the pain, He accepts this suffering out of love for all of us.

Jesus, help me to accept sacrifices in my life with love and patience. Teach me to trust in Your plan, even when it is difficult.

How can I offer love and patience during challenging times?

Station XII: Jesus Dies on the Cross

Jesus breathes His last on the cross, giving His life for the salvation of the world. His great sacrifice shows the depth of His love for us.

Jesus, thank You for Your sacrifice and endless love. Help me to remember Your gift of salvation and live my life in gratitude.

How can I show love and kindness to others in honor of Jesus' sacrifice?

Station XIII: Jesus Is Taken Down from the Cross

With love and tenderness, Jesus is carefully taken down from the cross by His friends and followers. This moment reminds us of the deep compassion and care shown to Him.

Jesus, help me to show kindness and care to others, especially those who are suffering. Teach me to be a source of comfort and love.

How can I offer compassion and help to someone in need today?

Station XIV: Jesus Is Laid in the Tomb

After His body is taken down from the cross, Jesus is lovingly placed in a tomb by His followers. They wrap Him in a clean cloth and roll a large stone to seal the entrance. It is a moment of sorrow, but also of hope, knowing that this is not the end.

Jesus, thank You for Your sacrifice and for showing us the way to eternal life. Help me to trust in Your promises, even in times of sadness and loss.

How can I show faith and hope, even in difficult moments?

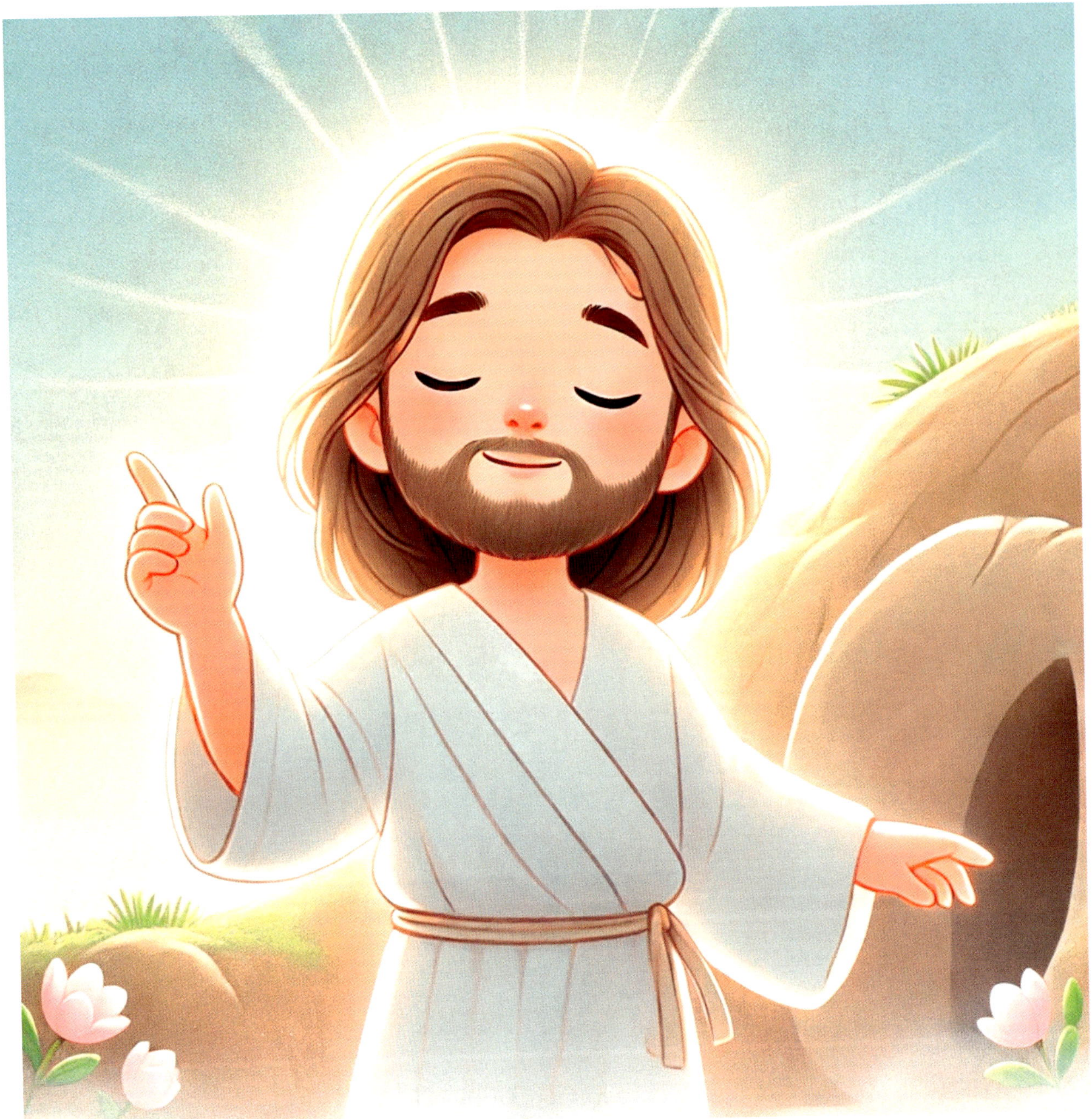

Made in the USA
Middletown, DE
04 March 2025